Lub Luffly

poems by Del Ray Cross

2006 : Pressed Wafer : Boston

for Curran, Yuki, and Otto

Poems in this book have appeared in
can we have our ball back?, *The Hat*, *Magazine Cypress*,
Shampoo, *Tinfish*, *the tiny*, and *VeRT*. A few came from
various *Postcard Poems* projects with Jim Behrle, Cassie Lewis,
Stephanie Young, and Tim Yu — some of these were published
by *Poetry Espresso*.

ISBN: 0-9785156-1-7
ISBN 13: 978-0-9785156-1-4

typeslowly designed

Cover art by Otto Chan

Printed in Michigan by Cushing-Malloy, Inc.

Pressed Wafer / 9 Columbus Square / Boston, MA 02116

Table of Contents

dimpled heart	9
Poems	10
the very idea	11
riot poem	12
Piano	14
Why so sulky?	15
postcard #2	16
presence	17
being	18
framed	19
the lyric is dead. long live the lyric.	20
A Valentine's Day Sonnet	21
unidentified sonnet	22
A Green Summer	23
nor legends (nor some stolen words)	25
the plan	26
a wave	27
portrait	29
Federico	31
"if u love #"	32
having been on the fence i was	33
shucks	34
The Sky Inside This Table	35
electronic handshake	37
A Time to Reap	38
I love you against the red bricks	39

anything about myself 41

It's a Bunch of People Trying to Make
a Mouth & It's a Long Dead Horse. 42

The Pacific 43

astral projection 45

at first 46

ludicrous construct (a poetics) 47

"Wednesday SYSCO truck on Calif" 48

anti-curmudgeon sonnet 49

your name 50

cathedral 51

intractable 52

interlude 53

it's too late for me 55

7 sins 56

"of the imaginary smokers" 59

hanashi 60

today 61

night and half-moons 62

or should i give myself a 63

i feel better every day i feel better 64

a cloud that interrupted 65

"I understand" 67

"u were saying" 68

"It is not right" 69

dove love 70

little list 71

square 72

Dear Stephanie,   73
On Friday Night   74
too many mosquitoes   76
for the last postcard poem   77
Carolina   78
I just wanna go to sleep   80
a kidney stone   81
LA thoughts   82
12 people on the way from the
    bathroom at the Abbey Cafe   83
after Hikmet   84
nostalgia   85
excerpts from afar east   86
Ways of Making Love   88
love poem (tentative title)   89
night train   91
if i am not here   92
i shd go thru this thing & take
    out snippets   93

dimpled heart

your knee moved nine times
toward the knuckles of my heart

no bird becomes a heart
without plastic scars

my poetry doesn't understand the heart
it requires an understanding of the heart

Poems

The hack of putting pen to paper
in order to park a record of existence
is a screwball comedy.
It's a nuisance and charms me.
A happy red blister on the thumb of my face.
I mean it's an instance,
like saying "I was here." Or more at
"I am here." No probably less at that.

The crack of writing is always an act.
"I write less words than I hues to."
Always the yellow road is less cold
with a bullet in my ink.
My poems are pretty good
when I have a nice transmission.
I drive through the crack like a distance,
scribbling little bruises into the median.
Tiny little ears of ink settle upon each tissue of flimflam
until there's a whole book of em.

I hack in order to park
on an instant. Sometimes even parallel,
which is great fun
and can often result in a haxident.

the very idea

as writers become more experimental
their finest poetry contains some sort
of narrative element. the work gener
ally hovers but they are experimental.
a moving fantastic wonderful piece
full of being choked to death. exper
imental and sensuous feminist poetry.
a precursor to the modern novel. gen
erously sprinkled with narrative tid
bits and massive amounts of keyword
poetry. lots of poems about murderers.
regional and psychological fiction. n
ovels dry humor drama and poetry
illustrative of software engineering.
more elements of character perform
ativity critical writing metaphor deb
ates on mythology characterization
dialogue memory imagery micro
fictions.

riot poem

written while studying Japanese
at the lake with no cellphone
bookstore, 8:01 p.m. (recapitulate)

throw rocks at the poets who make
no sense, buy a special pen
I called EVERYBODY

I know the garden is that way
under the cloud at the Elite Cafe
where the blues

my garden dress at 8:06
every week at 8:07 the blues
in the coffee of the expensive lake

my locksmith is better than
your locksmith
the little blue light flashes

you need architects with those
nest eggs
and a little memory

a star memory with perfume
which catches on fire
I have a friend who is on fire now

in most cases of the blues
I can't remember the boot
or the ship

this will happen with narration
it is clear at night
and chilly

everyone is smoking low to the
sidewalk (head low)
with no fireflies

Piano

We fumbled on the carpet
until the key slipped in, 2 a.m.
Dumbfounded, I covered up and
you got lost in the white shirts.

My hands sought more music,
played Brahms' *Liebeslieder Waltzes*,
two of four hands creating not enough
beautiful empty reminder of

hard wet teeth beneath soft lips.
That same night my hands so hungry
my breath covers a windshield until
I'm pulling somebody else's blond locks.

Music has wet my tongue and curled my
heart into a baffled bliss ever since.

Why so sulky?

Is writing music a recipe
for disaster?

Today we will try
sulky for the first time.

Can you see the
wet face in the movie?

The story ends in a
burst

immediately preceding
the pronunciations of

tripped, woodsplit,
and *candyass honeybuns.*

He was so cute
when he was sulky.

postcard #2

walk up top of Buena Vista
the sun on my neck is what'll I do
Chet Baker in my ears
honey-sweet but sounds like
a mouthful of marbles
"who's gonna make me gay now"
and he gets me hungry too
half-way up painted on a boulder
"oh grief love" skies o' blue
at the peak a smart little humming-
bird rests on top of a perky new tree
I rest too under a droopy eucalyptus
facing the north (my favorite)
Golden Gate Bridge and
blue paint on ash-bark that says
"Monday my damn man"

presence

my way of doing
all of this made me
close all the senses
and changed my heart
i was stunned by this

i've lost is feeling
pains a little present
knowing that u
think u touch
seeing your eyes

it is really important
watching me without
these memories i
actual got a little
present to grow up

being

being so close
seeing something
that is what has
change my heart

but different from
yours it's so dif
to keep me feeling
twice all i've told u

there are so many so
things i feel i have to
convince myself
but left a little

framed

so many there r
things i feel
like present

knowing that you
r doing important
sweet i fe

just wanted you to
*feel with almost
framed loving see

the lyric is dead. long live the lyric.

the go-go money
precludes any
dialogue
the tone is
many-tongued
syllablingbling
to correspond
to the insitutions
and to impress
an ear with its modulations
a collab genre
of sloppy listening
such as sonnet
fanatacism

A Valentine's Day Sonnet

Love is my one true specialty.
Even when I'm on the bus,
my heart pretends to bleed
and I'm thinking of you.

Cupid should've known better
than start a greeting card franchise.
Dearest you, I'm so in love.
Jewels from this pomegranate

ought to be squished by the
two arms of this Valentine's Day
card into something small and
sweet and red for you.

I've driven you numerous places
and painted your fingernails black.

unidentified sonnet

sistrum lupin contempt
chalcedony madrone
sorrel milch cress

oblique ruffian
brandish alder foreland
tether dibbling

reproachful turbid
fulvous wether keels
golondrina

wan cataract
draggled

A Green Summer

"Gay is, gay was, the gay forsythia ..."
                                    — Wallace Stevens

We seek a summer of green marble,
when consumer confidence and
inflation remain relatively muted.

A summer when I wonder if people in
Canada smoke more. The markets,
however, generally trail downwards.

Our summer of golf clubs is not
to the clouds' dismay — but the
forklift on the putting green is.

The weakest performing sectors
are utilities and health care. Once
again, I got lost in a thunderstorm.

Or we don't get them here, where
the U.S. dollar has weakened, relative
to peevish birds. No thunder whatsoever.

The federal funds rate is unchanged.
The best performing sectors are
the arts and consumer staples.

Also snow is something I no longer
know. This weakness enables
European and Japanese stocks.

I look across the hospital, over the webby
lamp. It's been two years and I have
yet to name the tree outside my window.

nor legends   (nor some stolen words)

(for Gerrit Lansing)

to be forgiven in the air
the whole seizure
bequeathed of new silhouettes
now dirty o dark breathless rhyme some night
blue sounds wrench
pop into blood the happy Charles
the wind in our heads

across the blinded avenue
in the filthy daylight roar
was a sexual blank-blank
it let in the spring
but you'd never soothe
the legendary dark elfs
lessen a wild secret, eh?

beautiful furry solace
against a drenched boulevard
the colors of hairy roses
near the sea's bailiwick

of love the change
of the sky what plunks
o don't try to get it all in

the plan

a booklength nonfiction
linear narrative
scoring randomly
generated angst

these novels have
still more limited
portholes the
surface offering

prose visual art
graphic freeverse
flash fiction
modernist whisk

I have been to
lunch and while
eating

a wave

large droplets fall from the eaves
of the boarded-up restaurant and onto
my blue shirt which is already warm as Herbert
short-circuits the blurred bricks rising from the
sidewalk that's just a puddle on the way to the bay

then when I place my face into the purple turquoise
parking meter an all-white thought bubble appears
that wants to say "Herbert stay right here" but
instead fills up with fog and crosses the
bridge into Oakland

I've seen Herbert ever since

Herbert who is special and now on my keyboard
which is the same as it's always been only a little more
dirty

Herbert who is only a fantasy or such a fresh mirage
that I cannot feel Herbert's results
except when Herbert looks up from the telephone
and lifts his thin hand into a half-wave

then it is very hard
for me to maintain the color of my wet shirt

it's such a tremendous feeling and the raindrops
only make it better

I love Herbert in my mind or in an
imaginary thunderstorm floating
into and out of my dream about the
Chinese Emperor in a gold-filigreed glass cage

portrait

a pouted mail
your beefed
desk beefs
a pouted mouth
of morning will
found them a
moon will
whistled will
one files were
not backed up
been beeping
a beeping mouth
wordered at it at a
beepered a
mouth can't
held how'd
you feel
talented hubris
a darkened dahlias
a darken birds
sung like
new black birds
that arrive
in the mail
eat breakfast

a strangle
not to talk
a stranger
eat breakfast
not to stranger
a taller nose
a talk strike

Federico

i am writing to
you from the
beyond
having found
a kiss that
will last the
equivalent
of 14 trees
m'god
o the lashes what
& no pantalones

if u love #
I will give u 3
then sleeping pills to fall

when we can frankly decide
the coolest thing going
somewhere suddenly

sunday afternoon or so
like making bluhbluh
then 2 hour nap evenings

with my body clock which is
kinda cruel for my body it's ok
        love love hyper and crazy

having been on the fence i was

having been on the fence i was
granted one celestial object. and his
mouth went into the steam. it so happens
it so happens it was a potato. so i put my
face into the fence and was brought
under the close control of government
scissors. a potato by no other name
remains a panic object or a panic
panic of self-description having been
granted a fence of no other steam.
it so happens when i went to mash
my face i was brought under the
control of the government. it bit me
by no other name. i put my face
into the face and it came out fresher.
it so happens a celestial potato
is under the close control of the.
self-description having been put. my
face. an abject panic. under which
there is no underwhich. because it just
happens i went to mash my face
and was brought under the control of
the government. it was one celestial
mouth.

shucks

full taxicab white giggle
that yellow with inline
silhouette of the umbrella
her hair is braided
yellow and blue! yesterday
in the shower some
earringed (upper right — the
new sexy way — you
know) tall slim brown
could not even tell
if it was a
smile trickle trickle the
water falls down on
me then it drops
into the drain slick
rainy sidewalks with three
taxicabs full of

The Sky Inside This Table

Angles enable the shortest
distance between two points.
Who is this other point?
My cup of coffee has ignited
and will soon be beamed elsewhere.

Do not squirm tepidly from those
distant days, that faded blueness.
That exhaust-filled blueness.
Golfers on couches resting their
heads. Poets drawing curtains.

A bird in the pie. Underneath this
pie is Lake Tahoe. Benign storms
coalesce, dumb beauty. These
angles are vain. Twenty times I've
gotten up to check myself in mirror.

Those distant days are anguished,
ravaged. White spiders latch onto
our skins and, dying, drying,
cling for months after. We finally
find them and wipe them off.

Not one to predict futures, the
giant lake melts. Rapidly, another
season gets eaten. I drink heavily.
One spot from the pine-clung catwalk
finds me, follows me for a moment,
then loses me.

electronic handshake

here's a story about how to
mix business with pleasure.
first nobody kisses nobody
on my roof while the fog
melts Sutro Tower.
but before I get to the roof
I tell many stories.
these are all true
from what I can tell.
later in the night
I ask Kevin how he
DOES everything.
I won't tell you the answer
because I don't believe it.

A Time to Reap

Investments in the bond market
were enjoyed with two margaritas
aimed at capitalizing on the Federal
blurry moon over Harvey's, whose
Reserve cut the interest rate and
expected the silent fiction
to reap considerable benefits on
the wall — "I've been this close
to the fourth-quarter earnings of
that actor," I said — he was a
regional bank like Comerica Inc.,
a twenty-one-year-old who'd had
robust gains which the industry
didn't eat but had covertly begun
to report. He was now performing
said substantional gains at the wall,
pretty lip dangling a Camel. He'd
used these gains to offset charges
in business lines and had already
bitten his red apple to the core.

I love you against the red bricks

your mouth is sort of open
and you wonder if I'm
breathing on you as
you lean against the
red bricks with your
mouth slightly open

I believe I could
find you easily
even though
it is a shame
you are not here
against the red
(orange and pink)
bricks which I
push you into
so hard

you don't want me to
and yet you let me

look at the socket
beneath your cheeks
aqua blue
which the spotlight lights

where the paintings
are supposed to be

where you lean
slightly against your
open mouth
and its red bricks
so discordant

anything about myself

though my heart
is tumbled down
but all hooked up
let's write his name again

featuring this morning

one of those
impressive
verysingle

a mostimportant
person followed by
wehadlunch
rentedamovie
walkedaround and
foundamansion

It's a Bunch of People Trying to Make a Mouth & It's a Long Dead Horse.

Whenever I sleep, or these last
few days, my head becomes the
shape of a tangerine and I wake
myself up with a burning tongue.

Burning tongue disease.

I didn't know either of them
and I'm not an anthropologist
(Hold on, this makes sense).

He's drinking a mojito
with a very nice ass
(This is narrative).

I could quilt everything into a narrative, but then
would I still have a crush on the coat-check guy?

Because I kissed him
next to the pool table once.
I'm certain he remembers.
Why have an obsession
when there are so many other ways
to hate our president?

She's such a beautiful James Dean.

The Pacific

I am a sexual predator.
The waves see smoke and rise up to meet it.
Small droplets of rain on a sea of rocks.
Rubbing against the leaves of a baby gingko.

Two trashcans next to a puddle.
A lanky guy in a fleece jacket walks by.
An airplane flies over another man who's inspecting a rock.
A mollusk. A rock. A mollusk. A rock.

The lanky guy stops at my car.
Unshaven a few days he balances on a dead phone pole.
A curb to keep cars from drowning.
He balances in his corduroys. Gray but greener than the water.

The ocean water.
Tearing at the rocks.
A tour bus arrives and the lanky guy cowers into the woods.
Frightened by the tourists.

But not before teetering on the pole, peering down into my
                    windshield.
Asking me maybe if I'd like a blow.
An old man and an old woman pose for a camera.
They stand next to the gingko and wait for the flash.

I'm not shaking anymore as the profound geese fly from
                    right to left.
Out over the gray waters where a big boat flickers.
Some crack in the cloud a hummingbird uses.
Hummingbird portraiture.

I am the most desirable tree on this beach.
Nobody lands on me but for a second.
My roots are steep and poisoned by this earth's trappings.
A wind has come and blown me over. And blown me over.

astral projection

the writing is clear and narrative.
i can't write with my hands.
too much tug of war.
compared with the poet's use
of language the dead leaves
are stirring up too much pass
ionately. the myths are not
interested in language. it's
looking pretty bad so i'm sitt
ing in the middle of the trail
with the black ants.

at first

i bent and found
the lampshade had worn thin.
to kiss a tongue slide almond
one hundred thirty five degrees i
bent and. at first i felt. this
was second. to slide a tongue.
forthmouth haven't. our achy kneads.
i fall upon a. was forced into
the lampshade had worn thin. i felt
a rapid. i found forthwith a rising
motionfunction. a lambshade one third twisted i
i thirty five function. tongue slide
slick an almond colored dark a rise.
had worn thin. forthcoming. one sex
glows beyond another.

ludicrous construct (a poetics)

That's my therapy couch
quote of the day.
       (seriously)
             Feeling
old hat. Where's my sex
appeal? My thought is
a haircut. Or I'm just
quirkyalone. All I can
tell you is there's
something to do
and something exists.

Wednesday SYSCO truck on Calif
ornia dithers. Taxi plunges into
a cigarette. Fourteen mochas later
this guy's plugged into something.
His ear with all the wires. {Gypsy
moths and cedar ashes.} Psycholo
gy is finished at Cingular Wireless.
Open the floodgates on my raunchy
hot dog t-shirt. A month of ele
gance is what it gets you. Four
bamboos on wheels roll by with
hyacinths. I swear there's nowhere
to end this. But then I lean over
and smell your bleaches.

anti-curmudgeon sonnet

I will not be a jerk.
I will not be a jerk.
I will not be a jerk.
I will not be a jerk.
I will not be a jerk.
I will not be a jerk.
I will not be a jerk.
I will not be a jerk.
I will not be a jerk.
I will not be a jerk.
I will not be a jerk.
I will not be a jerk.
I will not be a jerk.
I will not be a jerk.

your name

looks
Gorgeous
Lily

think
world
isn't

have
savings
flowers

and
ice
cream

cathedral

butter-clad branches
dry the tears it takes to
send an orange bloom
through the internet

they reach into the
sky for years and
what does the sky
bring them but
martins and such

while the same
butterflies move
from story
to story

intractable

if you want me to
buy my phone number
and show up on the
sawhorse at one o'clock
where you smoke hearts
i'll just fall into that guy
on the parquet and _look_
i'm behind in language
my vanilla is pencil
lisa the tuesday
please gimme what loves for now
the olive seven seas

interlude

skies fly into my mouth as you walk up Grant Ave
a kind of sky in my head whom satin dresses
over the date palms under which he's walking
I wonder

the red sky placed its hand on my shoulder
a kind of sun in my head whose pleated skirt
blown by the wind in my heart that has a fly
swallowed

I love in my heart the orange that I want him to wear
a pleated skirt whose head is a heart a kind of sky
blown by the wind with flag-driven wonder its drive
unrepentant

when my head was dissolving you were walking up
Grant Ave you had just placed your cheek against
mine and a sudden whiff had drifted in through
the window

my knowledge does not equal my heart it does not
find its way into my head like the clouds through
which airplanes and their pleated skirts a fly
swallowed

the time which is now I love your walking up
Grant Ave and back to my cheek where in my
head a sun is dissolving your shoulder a brilliant
orange pleated skirt blown by the wind

thank you red noise
thank you sunfly
thank you brick wall
thank you love in my head you were walking

it's too late for me

honestly, you don't have to grow up, little
fish of the pinched lip. instead, simply
eat your worm. (my, how the snuggle is
mistranslated.) simply eat your fish as
others worm their way into senility. you
don't have to grow up. simply unfurl.
don't struggle as a means to be literal. little
worm, you can always be an earlybird.
bird, fish, or little worm, find your way to
senseless. fish for it. yearn to learn for
nothing. fly around in circles. call upon the
swelling stars. see to it, early fish, early
worm, see to it that you fly literally into the
group. a grouper you are. my what an
early bird, fish full of minutes and
never another day. find your way to
nothing. what is a child, fishes, fishes,
skies, skies? what catches the worm in its
limpid craw? don't be guilty limping fish.
so you didn't grow up. didn't get grown.
what a nerve. you didn't get grown up
and don't. never.

7 sins

pride

the flowers i gave you
are the ones i picked.

the mountain where
i picked them …

what lovely peacocks there.
each flower i picked
one flew away.

envy

the ship sails off before
the stench leaves the bay.

i watch it go.

i was in love with the water
that brought that ship to me.

gluttony

the fish looked at me.
the fish looked at my friend.
we both ate the fish.

after we ate the fish
we ate some more fish.
and then we drank some warm green tea.

lust

somebody got between
you and me. a handsome face
with a handsome body.
we glued ourselves to
the face and body. and
then we squeezed.
until it was just us again.

anger

happiness is a walk
along the water.

the many flowers
are beautiful there.

you kicked me first.
i kissed your bloody lip.

greed

i followed him
to the top of the city.
i picked up each scrap
he left behind.
somehow i lost him.
now his toys will not
disappear from the horizon.

sloth

each time i tried
to pick myself up

    another house
    fell on top of me.

of the imaginary smokers
I remember this hunk of sound
    (fuu)
was a disproportionate secret
its two smokes and I was
high school kisses too comf
ortable on his lips or the
moles near his safety pins
oh I tried to date him to
listen to what he can hear
    (clasps ears)
if only he were still here
    (ah here he is smoking
    an imaginary cigarette)
I am dancing next to the
part in his hair

hanashi

While we talk
I'm not gonna
talk about
me or you.

A new sky
is formed
upon the
words we

don't use.
Two pillows
raised to it,
and a laugh

that starts in
one throat
and ends
in another.

today

today being somewhat
daydreams of the legs
on my neck

is being a waterfallen
molf of what is around
the bend of your ear

is being to understand
the purple of the night
or the lock of the maw

or the mwamwa that is
out of the molf of your
molf a movement

by the way sound's
like nothing can sound
like wa like I wah

all inside a button-up
that's ringing what
today's muffle is like

today of course being
somewhat unburdged
and unforzen

night and half-moons

half-moons at night
see themselves opening up
out of the ground
as windows blaze pinkish flesh
and stars wave their tails
the little charcoals that burn the night
the night with no bull's-eye
it's too long
even the dark birds splash across the sky
with no sound that can disturb someone
the stars peeping in solace
and now all the blurred movement
above the billboards and breakdowns

or should i give myself a

i've revamped the fog. the turf tongue
clouds and the how's it been thirteen
years since we. and i dreamed
disingenuous dreams no trees a.
cathedral of earth. unopened oh
why don't you just open it. when
i met the car. i'd revamped the fog
turf. go for broke. when a good poet
dies ingenuity. a little boy a little
orange boat on the gray bay cloudful.
a demented yellow truck a sailboat.
the surface of the bay like a map.
turquoise ashtray gray violet astroturf
globecolored homogeny. is not
for us. mono a nono. where this is
heading ashram. this automatic add up.
this stolen flag from south dakota.
many red apartment buildings.

i feel better every day i feel better

i feel better every day i feel better.
i don't like pain is a four-letter word is
a bird climbing over an evergreen shrub.
are you a bottom or a top?
i'm romantic sitting in a little corner.
people come and go they come and
go and i'm romantic. the way you
love me and you and you and the
bird climbing over an evergreen shrub.
i feel better every day is a four-letter
word is a four-letter word.

a cloud that interrupted

we kiss like with
chainsaws and jackhammers
under a blue to which
horseflies go.

your hoodwinked
thieves are hidden
behind the sofa. but you
are such a lovely long body

under the green.
the same fuzzy face
behind yellow petals.
a face behaving like a

television which i'll accept it.
like a television i turned off
all the other lights, emptied
the reservoir under my

lamp which is this loneliness.
every dining room
i remembered in my head
was lost, disposed of

properly while a
seagull,
its left leg my own,
however weaker.

i said i wanted to
crawl back into
bed with you
this morning

and i really really
meant it to be so,
but these things
are every one leaving us,

like socks or church bells
or passive clouds,
so as to become
a violent nostalgia.

I understand
u attend many poetry
and bunch of friends
but I am kinda thinking
next weekend sweetdreams
which is 22nd and 23rd
I may be at home
reading as I do for dancing
carry some music with u
it's a chance I could be tired
but I wake u up 7:30
hehehe
I come back home
5am and sleep plenty with u

u were saying
I went downtown
for covering up guy
which I take offensive

don't cancel your gym
between songs I just
refill your energy

hope u r having
good time being tourist

in a red jeep
where u love me

A poet only writes poems.
That is all he should have to do.
— John Wieners

It is not right
for the sun
to shine.

Maybe this fucking tight knot
in my stomach
is unraveling.

Where is the
source of the
pain?

dove love

it's a sunshine blue day
a car alarm sounds
briefly
i turn a corner & there're
3 doves clumped together
in the shade of a hedgerow
it's almost autumn
1 flies away
to a brick circle nearby
where there's also a horsefly
& a trashcan standing in the shade
the other 2 doves look 'in love'
maybe all 3 are in love
with each other

little list

corner of Sanchez & 21st

hilltop
white butterfly
4 fogs
neither wistful nor lonely
"that's the dream"
biker ogles
faraway big air conditioners
"twick twickle"
Cabriolet
rose leaves
some purple
shadows
ants

square

the fog has burnt mostly
the tiles on the ceiling
like styrofoam they hold
in some of the noise
big boats out the window
look like islands on the blue bay
the whiteboards need to be erased
i'm having trouble with stuff
but i won't write a poem about it
i took a nap on the couch
in the office and this i do
on occasion

Dear Stephanie,

I just returned from directing a movie
on location in Lisbon.

I just returned from Hong Kong where
I had a victorious business meeting.

I just returned from the Amazon.

Then I landed a gig as a covert swabbie
on a Pacific cruise vessel.

I just returned from Alaska where I
killed a few bears.

I just married a princess during a
hot air balloon ride.

These are just some of the things
that I have recently enjoyed.

On Friday Night

On Friday night I walked alone
through the cool air. It was comfortable.
A woman several floors up called
down to me: "Are you Kyle?"
I'd never seen her before. And then
some guy stopped me, asked me to
give him a slow massage; he was
six feet two inches tall
with beautiful lemony skin.
I'd never given a massage to a
stranger before. He led me to his
apartment and said that I was too shy,
that I should climb on top of him.
He was ready with oils. He'd lit several
candles and selected some music.
Afterwards, I walked back down
Baker Street, and looked up to
the woman who was still leaning
out her window. "Oh, come on,
you're Kyle aren't you?" I stopped
long enough to reply that I was
not the man she was waiting for.
When I got home I skimmed through
my grandmother's old scrapbook for
the first time. It was full of

newspaper clippings, mostly of men killed in action during World War II. It was her birthday.

too many mosquitoes

hello from aptos. i'm congested.
when one loses language one
loses a. this might be read as
narrative or as a trail of black
ants and children screaming.
prose is narrative. all poetry
is fragment. bugs.
toothbrush archive.
a bug died on my glasses.
now i have to bike uphill.
hurry up. and while you're looking
you've got to rhythm metaphor
lines stanzas lyricism.

for the last postcard poem

the literary object
this game of Ackerengendered
formalizing of the information saga
as related disciples & dramatic structure
videofilm collaboratives effective
ly editing and writing becomes less
true as writers put spoons through
communication chambers of axe
Mediterranean memory Korean
narrative gone hopefully to have
miscellaneous love poems
twisted and therefore falling
fallingfalling fallingfalling
there's a spoon around his neck
can you see it?

Carolina

during our conversation
on the palette which was
so impulsive and about
our future everything
was too soft and we held onto the eaves
like a secret

a twitter of affirmation
flew by the window
it was something
like a bird at four in the morning
I noticed this
in such a gentle way
as if it were an affectionate hand-clasp
before we had to saddle up
and choke upon all our
hopes

soon
we were led down
into a moonlit cove
the ocean at our shoulders
was a constance that kept
bucketing our words
and pouring them back into
our mouths

where we held onto them
with salt-soaked tongues
until we couldn't taste
or talk

I just wanna go to sleep

The Britons have handed in
their butter-tickets, and we've
windswept notions, ravines
within the intellect, the fog,
desiccated feathers of peahen,
heather, that've all been shaved,
scattered. Sea-bounced hair
and unearthly eyes, nearly
closing into their sharpened
elbows. Water-pipes, fitted,
everywhere — see the gray.
I've written all this before,
oil from banged-up bowls
and jars of leaves. Like the
after-image on a dark monitor,
sure as a swallow on a gray-green
pole, or a thick-lisped grackle
breathing heavily into a mike.
Are you there, forty winks? If
so, dream of an underlying dance,
where all the weather rains upon
pizza joints, each drowsing in
the blue drizzle, sodden castles.
The cow, only a home to the
cat, who slips out of the wool
onto her flak jacket, lamp,
thistle, sheepskin, sleep.

a kidney stone

It was so tiny,
your kidney stone.
When I woke up
with appendicitis
I had no insurance.
The ER doctor
sent me home with
a stomach virus
and suppositories
to dull the pain.
A nurse's aide asks,
"Is that a mohawk?"
You've thrown up
from the Demoral
(after 5 useless shots
of morphine), but it
helped, thank God.
One man a few doors
down from us screams
so loudly you wince
through the fog
of your medication;
you're in so much pain,
but it soon passes.

LA thoughts

just past Buttonwillow where I saw
the ghost on the side of the road

scribbling "odd boulders" onto the
back of the map

echoes of the bartender
who looked like Jon Bon Jovi

and the man at The Revolver
who kept applauding the television set

little green earthworm-looking smudge
on the gigantic David Hockney painting

so I call my mother who has yet to receive
her Scandal, Inc. with Robert Hutton

12 people on the way from the bathroom at The Abbey Cafe

1. coffee top bongo
2. orange cap
3. wipe eyebrows
4. do waiters count?
5. pull up pants
6. put on apron
7. "I've walked by 4 times"
8. fast as I can go
9. with a beer bottle
10. flannel will get you everywhere
11. he doesn't love me
12. he does

after Hikmet

all I wrote about us is lies
the enchanted arbor was just a
    brow-furrowing denseness
    clogged with fallen time
your peculiar traipsing through
    snowfall like Frankenstein's
    monster's
unreal
a faraway blanket of daffodil petals
    approximating snowfall
    has fallen onto thick mud
and you're stuck
maybe sinking
a river moaning "springtime"
    in the distance as the ice breaks
and you'd hear it all
    with your soft, blood-pink ears
    if only you had them
I close my eyes and watch you
    walk into the snowstorm

nostalgia

several girls in orange dresses
run with multi-colored umbrellas
through a field of black blooms

tall trees are blown westward
where they steep in the shadows
of red barns and silos

the windblown girls trample
the black blooms — they run red
as the barns red like strawberries

next to the buttercup birdbath
yellow as the swaying birdhouses
the girls are running like sunset

in their bright orange dresses
they run with big white umbrellas
and trample the sky-colored blooms

excerpts from afar east

oh my dear
I am so sorry
that I could not
hit on this way
in full order
to give you
the file
from yesterday
which was
such a rush

as we have been
tight-lipped and
much one-upped

but I did manage
to unzip yours
with fanfare
and found
how rosy
you are
always
to me

thanks bales
for this
lovely grain
of lump
that you
did deliver
with such
an open palm
and made my day

Ways of Making Love

1. Lying in bed, listening to somebody walk up and down the stairs.

2. Who's that closing the door?

3. After you ordered a Scotch and then disappeared.

4. This is what they call a "hard San Francisco rain."

5. Take a slow walk through a long park.

6. Next to a urinal.

7. On a deer-stand in an old oak tree with a shotgun apiece.

8. I keep looking at you, sipping hot coffee.

9. Remember what happened in the arboretum.

10. At night, smoking on the roof, with a very nice view of the city.

love poem (tentative title)

It's raining on California and the
umbrellas aren't what they used to be.
The fancy pants and leather jackets are getting sopped.

All the oranges in the cafe have soured a little bit
and I'm watching your eyes flit
between the sogged sleeping bags and the museum.

There's also that long strand of reddened hair over your right ear,
my left,
put there when your lips left their mug

and floated over the luxury apartment building.
Oh and that's when I investigated the peculiar
shape of your chest from Monterey.

How you are breathing during this rainstorm!
Over the grated orange rinds that float atop your coffee
in its fancy cup on my mother's birthday in 2004.

When I look up to where the sky is the rain washes my eyes out
and it's like my shoes are still untied at Macy's and I'm reading
poems on t-shirts while you swiftly shift from rack to rack.

But anyway there's still no thunder in San Francisco.
And there's really nothing outstanding but the low-hung clouds
reveling in — I mean reliving — our every last argument.

night train

what are you thinking tonight
as no stars shine down upon Iowa
do you think perhaps we could reverse course
and make more fireplaces out of cellos
like you take one end of the spaghetti and I'll take the other
is it good that I've left two frosted glasses on the teakwood table
next to the butcher's block
one with a big blood-red bloom thrust upright
into the babies'-breath blown out the other

let the waters in each glass sweeten for a thousand miles or so
until the instant before the light behind the paper lampshade fades
or the moon gets lost over Nebraska
then take a pair of chopsticks out of the kitchen drawer
and let the train disappear into smoke
tap ta-tap ta-tap ta-tap
into smoke that gets lost in the night as it blackens
and smothers all other noises
is rich and warm as a cello stuck inside a hide-a-bed

if i am not here

i can't form complete thoughts
everything to mean am i mucking
as nothing i say write it's special
stressing no longer have my life
not poetry people like who they
already have it plagued with doubt
nor creative time is not poetry

i shd go thru this thing & take out snippets

a concentrated and heightened
form of language. can't i just
sit here and count butterflies?
my cellphone has no reception.
this leads to a greater
construction of narrative
character development cohe
sion. someone will point out
how this is the finest poetry
i've ever eggtossed. i
would tell you something
about myself if i knew.